A Heart for God

Inspiration for Moms

A Heart for God

Inspiration for Moms

Adapted from *Bible Wisdom for Mothers*
by Gary Wilde

Compiled by Mark R. Littleton

Victor Books is an imprint of ChariotVictor Publishing, a division of Cook Communications,
Colorado Springs, Colorado 80918
Cook Communications, Paris, Ontario
Kingsway Communications, Eastbourne, England

3 4 5 6 7 8 9 10 Printing/Year 01 00 99 98

Introduction

What is a mother to do? She must make the beds, dress the children, satisfy her husband, please her boss, and walk with Christ, every day, always, for the rest of her life.

Is it any wonder she feels wrung-out, tired, whipped, burnt out and up?

In at least one area here is help. What you will find in these pages will overflow into all other areas, enabling a mother to face life dauntless and full of hope.

Why?

Unlike some other gift books that contain good man-made words, this book serves up only great God-made words, the very Word of God from the Bible. Every page in this book contains a nugget of God's Word, using several wonderful translations. Mothers will enjoy reading this book on a daily basis as part of their devotions or just to get a palmful of insight for a passle of problems.

Read these words and be filled with hope, mothers. God speaks today as He did so long ago, and the power of His words has not diminished.

God's assurance to His people:

Though an army besiege me, my heart will not fear; though war break out against me, even then I will be confident (Ps. 27:3, NIV).

Counsel to the ambitious:

I returned and saw under the sun that the race is not to the swift, nor the battle to the strong, nor bread to the wise, nor riches to men of understanding. Nor favor to men of skill; but time and chance happen to them all. For man also does not know his time; like fish taken in a cruel net, like birds caught in a snare, so the sons of men are snared in an evil time, when it falls suddenly upon them (Ecc. 9:11-12, NKJV).

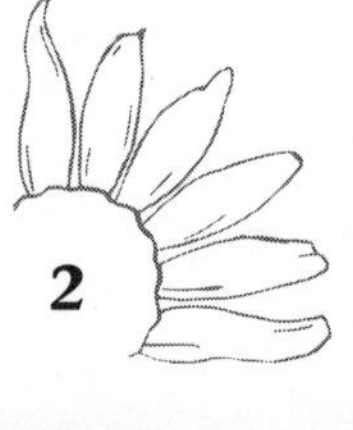

God is with us:

Be strong and of a good courage, fear not, nor be afraid of them; for the Lord thy God, he it is that doth go with thee; he will not fail thee, nor forsake thee (Deut 31:6).

Where to look for help:

I lift up my eyes to the hills—from where will my help come? My help comes from the Lord, who made heaven and earth. He will not let your foot be moved; he who keeps you will not slumber. He who keeps Israel will neither slumber nor sleep.The Lord is your keeper; the Lord is your shade at your right hand. The sun shall not strike you by day, nor the moon by night. The Lord will keep you from all evil; he will keep your life. The Lord will keep your going out and your coming in from this time on and forevermore (Ps. 121:1-8, NRSV).

About our fears:

Therefore we will not fear, though the earth should change, and though the mountains be shaken into the midst of the sea (Ps. 46:3, AMP).

God cares for us:

Are not five sparrows sold for two cents? And yet not one of them is forgotten by God. Indeed the very hairs of your head are all numbered. Do not fear; you are of more value than many sparrows (Luke 12:6-8, NASB).

We are part of God's kingdom:

Do not be afraid, little flock, for your Father has been pleased to give you the kingdom (Luke 12:32, NIV).

The Great Inner Resource:

For God has not given us a spirit of fear, but of power and of love and of a sound mind (2 Tim. 1:7, NKJV).

On fears and anxieties:

Be careful for nothing; but in everything by prayer and supplication with thanksgiving let your request be made known unto God. And the peace of God, which passeth all understanding, shall keep your hearts and minds through Christ Jesus (Phil. 4:6-7).

God's closeness to the hurting:

The Lord is near to the brokenhearted, and saves the crushed in spirit (Ps. 34:18, NRSV).

God's ability to provide emotional and spiritual health to His people:

He heals the brokenhearted, and binds up their wounds (Ps. 147:3, NASB).

A woman's triumphant song:

Then the prophet Miriam, Aaron's sister, took a tambourine in her hand; and all the women went out after her with tambourines and with dancing. And Miriam sang to them: "Sing to the Lord, for he has triumphed gloriously; horse and rider he has thrown into the sea" (Ex. 15:20-21, NRSV).

A word of praise:

Then Deborah and Barak the son of Abinoan sang on that day, saying, "When leaders lead in Israel, when the people willingly offer themselves, bless the Lord! Hear, O kings! Give ear, O princes! I, even I, will sing to the Lord; I will sing praise to the Lord God of Israel" (Jud. 5:1-3, NKJV).

Even the lost can hear the voice of God:

And while he was sitting on the judgment seat, his wife sent to him, saying, "Have nothing to do with that righteous Man; for last night I suffered greatly in a dream because of Him" (Matt. 27:19, NASB).

Women were some of Jesus' most committed followers:

Among them were Mary Magdalene, Mary the mother of James and Joseph, and the mother of Zebedee's sons. As evening approached, there came a rich man from Arimathea, named Joseph, who had himself become a disciple of Jesus. Going to Pilate, he asked for Jesus' body, and Pilate ordered that it be given to him. Joseph took the body, wrapped it in a clean linen cloth, and placed it in his own new tomb that he had cut out of the rock. He rolled a big stone in front of the entrance to the tomb, and went away. Mary Magdalene and the other Mary were sitting there across from the tomb (Matt. 27:56-61, NIV).

Women walked with Jesus through His darkest days:

Near the cross of Jesus stood his mother, his mother's sister, Mary the wife of Clopas, and Mary of Magdala (John 19:25, NIV).

Women have always been counted among Jesus' stoutest supporters:

And when he had considered the thing, he came to the house of Mary the mother of John, whose surname was Mark; where many were gathered together praying (Acts 12:12).

A new convert opens her home to the apostles:

A certain woman named Lydia, a worshiper of God, was listening to us; she was from the city of Thyatira and a dealer in purple cloth. The Lord opened her heart to listen eagerly to what was said by Paul. When she and her household were baptized, she urged us, saying, "If you have judged me to be faithful to the Lord, come and stay at my home." And she prevailed upon us (Acts 16:14-15, NRSV).

True servants of Christ:

I commend to you our sister Phoebe, who is a servant of the church which is at Cenchrea; that you receive her in the Lord in a manner worthy of the saints, and that you help her in whatever matter she may have need of you; for she herself has also been a helper of many, and of myself as well (Rom. 16:1-2, NASB).

A prayer to start the day:

Let the words of my mouth and the meditation of my heart be acceptable in Your sight, O Lord, my [firm, impenetrable] rock and redeemer (Ps. 19:14, AMP).

Avoid this:

The woman Folly is loud; she is undisciplined and without knowledge (Prov. 9:13, NIV).

Pass on the faith to your children:

For I am mindful of the sincere faith within you, which first dwelt in your grandmother Lois, and your mother Eunice, and I am sure that it is in you as well (2 Tim. 1:5, NASB).

Grace, the mark of a wise woman:

A gracious woman retaineth honour; and strong men retain riches (Prov. 11:16).

On beauty and wisdom:

Like a gold ring in a pig's snout is a beautiful woman without good sense (Prov. 11:22, NRSV).

What to do in your home:

The wise woman builds her house, but the foolish pulls it down with her hands (Prov. 14:1, NKJV).

God's gift to men:

Houses and riches are an inheritance from fathers, but a prudent wife is from the Lord (Prov. 19:14, NKJV).

Don't be contentious:

A continual dripping on a very rainy day and a contentious woman are alike (Prov. 27:15, NKJV).

A soon-to-be mother's cry of joy:

Mary said, "My soul praises the Lord and my spirit rejoices in God my Savior, for he has been mindful of the humble state of his servant. From now on all generations will call me blessed, for the Mighty One has done great things for me—holy is his name. His mercy extends to those who fear him, from generation to generation. He has performed mighty deeds with his arm; he has scattered those who are proud in the inmost thoughts. He has brought down rulers from their thrones but has lifted up the humble. He has filled the hungry with good things but has sent the rich away empty. He has helped his servant Israel, remembering to be merciful to Abraham and his descendants forever, even as he said to our fathers" (Luke 1:46-55, NIV).

A woman's commitment:

There was also a prophet, Anna the daughter of Phanuel, of the tribe of Asher. She was of a great age, having lived with her husband seven years after her marriage, then as a widow to the age of eighty-four. She never left the temple, but worshiped there with fasting and prayer night and day. At that moment she came, and began to praise God and to speak about the child to all who were looking for the redemption of Jerusalem (Luke 2:36-38, NRSV).

On sin:

Who can understand his errors? Cleanse thou me from secret faults. Keep back thy servant also from presumptuous sins; let them not have dominion over me; then I shall be upright, and I shall be innocent from the great transgression. Let the words of my mouth, and the meditation of my heart, be acceptable in thy sight, O Lord, my strength, and my redeemer (Ps. 19:14-16).

Jesus' invitation to His people:

Come to Me, all you who labor and are heavy laden, and I will give you rest. Take My yoke upon you and learn from Me, for I am gentle and lowly in heart, and you will find rest for your souls. For My yoke is easy and My burden is light (Matt. 11:28-30, NKJV).

Be honest in the dark and in the light:

There is nothing concealed that will not be disclosed, or hidden that will not be made known. What you have said in the dark will be heard in the daylight, and what you have whispered in the ear in the inner rooms will be proclaimed from the housetops (Luke 12:2-3, NIV).

A place to go for the thirsty:

Now on the last day, the great day of the feast, Jesus stood and cried out, saying, "If any man is thirsty, let him come to Me and drink. He who believes in Me, as the Scripture said, 'From his innermost being shall flow rivers of living water' " (John 7:37-38, NASB).

The way of salvation for all:

If you confess with your mouth Jesus as Lord, and believe in your heart that God raised Him from the dead, you shall be saved; for with the heart man believes, resulting in righteousness, and with the mouth he confesses, resulting in salvation (Rom. 10:9-10, NASB).

goal:

The wise woman builds her house, but with her own hands the foolish one tears hers down (Prov. 14:1, NIV).

A truly great woman:

A capable wife who can find? She is far more precious than jewels. The heart of her husband trusts in her, and he will have no lack of gain. She does him good, and not harm, all the days of her life.... Her children rise up and call her happy; her husband too, and he praises her: "Many women have done excellently, but you surpass them all." Charm is deceitful, and beauty is vain, but a woman who fears the Lord is to be praised. Give her a share in the fruit of her hands, and let her works praise her in the city gates (Prov. 31:10-12, 28-31, NRSV).

A husband on his wife's beauties:

How beautiful you are, my darling, how beautiful you are! Your eyes are like doves behind your veil; your hair is like a flock of goats that have descended from Mount Gilead. Your teeth are like a flock of newly shorn ewes which have come up from their washing, all of which bear twins, and not one among them has lost her young. Your lips are like a scarlet thread, and your mouth is lovely. Your temples are like a slice of pomegranate behind your veil. Your neck is like the tower of David built with rows of stones, on which are hung a thousand shields, all the round shields of the mighty men. Your two breasts are like two fawns, twins of a gazelle, which feeds among the lilies. Until the cool of the day when the shadows flee away, I will go my way to the mountain of myrrh and to the hill of frankincense (Song 4:1-7, NASB).

Even small things count in God's eyes:

I tell you the truth, anyone who gives you a cup of water in my name because you belong to Christ will certainly not lose his reward (Mark 9:41, NIV).

On giving:

I have shown you all things, how that so labouring ye ought to support the weak, and to remember the words of the Lord Jesus, how he said, It is more blessed to give than to receive (Acts 20:35).

On hospitality:

Contribute to the needs of God's people—sharing in the necessities of the saints—pursuing the practice of hospitality (Rom. 12:13, AMP).

On helping:

Suppose a brother or sister is without clothes and daily food. If one of you says to him, "Go, I wish you well; keep warm and well fed," but does nothing about his physical needs, what good is it? (James 2:15-16, NIV)

Open your home to others:

Be hospitable to one another without grumbling. As each one has received a gift, minister it to one another, as good stewards of the manifold grace of God (1 Peter 4:9-10, NKJV).

Have you been visited by an angel?

Do not neglect to show hospitality to strangers, for by this some have entertained angels without knowing it (Heb. 13:2, NASB).

Avoid quarrels:

An ally offended is stronger than a city; such quarreling is like the bars of a castle (Prov. 18:19, NRSV).

A sad state:

It is better to dwell in a corner of the housetop, than with a brawling woman in a wide house (Prov. 21:9).

prayer:

May the God who gives endurance and encouragement give you a spirit of unity among yourselves as you follow Christ Jesus, so that with one heart and mouth you may glorify the God and Father of our Lord Jesus Christ (Rom. 15:5-6, NIV).

On burdens:

Bear one another's burdens, and so fulfill the law of Christ. For if anyone thinks himself to be something, when he is nothing, he deceives himself. But let each one examine his own work, and then he will have rejoicing in himself alone, and not in another (Gal. 6:2-4, NKJV).

On unity:

I, therefore, the prisoner in the Lord, beg you to lead a life worthy of the calling to which you have been called, with all humility and gentleness, with patience, bearing with one another in love, making every effort to maintain the unity of the Spirit in the bond of peace (Eph. 4:1-3, NRSV).

Grow up!

Then we will no longer be infants, tossed back and forth by the waves, and blown here and there by every wind of teaching and by the cunning and craftiness of men in their deceitful scheming. Instead, speaking the truth in love, we will in all things grow up into him who is the Head, that is, Christ. From him the whole body, joined and held together by every supporting ligament, grows and builds itself up in love, as each part does its work (Eph. 4:14-16, NIV).

On the Spirit:

And do not get drunk with wine, in which is dissipation; but be filled with the Spirit, speaking to one another in psalms and hymns and spiritual songs, singing and making melody in your heart to the Lord, giving thanks always for all things to God the Father in the name of our Lord Jesus Christ (Eph. 5:18-20, NKJV).

A legacy:

Know therefore that the Lord thy God, he is God, the faithful God, which keepeth covenant and mercy with them that love him and keep his commandments to a thousand generations (Deut. 7:9).

The way to success:

This book of the law shall not depart out of thy mouth; but thou shalt meditate therein day and night, that thou mayest observe to do according to all that is written therein; for then thou shalt make thy way prosperous, and then thou shalt have good success (Josh. 1:8).

What to think about:

I will meditate also upon all Your work and consider all Your [mighty] deeds (Ps. 77:12, AMP).

Alone at night:

When I remember Thee on my bed, I meditate on Thee in the night watches (Ps. 63:6, NASB).

On dreams:

Delight yourself in the Lord and he will give you the desires of your heart (Ps. 37:4, NIV).

A promise:

The Lord preserves all those who love Him, but all the wicked will He destroy (Ps. 145:20, AMP).

Wisdom's cry:

I love those who love me, and those who seek me diligently find me (Prov. 8:17, NRSV).

The proof of our love for God:

He who has My commandments and keeps them, he it is who loves Me; and he who loves Me shall be loved by My Father, and I will love him, and disclose Myself to him (John 14:21, NASB).

How to look at your husband:

My beloved is white and ruddy, chief among ten thousand. His head is like the finest gold; his locks are wavy, and black as a raven. His eyes are like doves by the rivers of waters, washed with milk, and fitly set. His cheeks are like a bed of spices, banks of scented herbs. His lips are lilies, dripping liquid myrrh. His hands are rods of gold set with beryl. His body is carved ivory inlaid with sapphires. His legs are pillars of marble set on bases of fine gold. His countenance is like Lebanon, excellent as the cedars. His mouth is most sweet, yes, he is altogether lovely. This is my beloved, and this is my friend, O daughters of Jerusalem! (Song 5:10-16, NKJV)

Commands for a wife and husband:

But to the married I give instructions, not I, but the Lord, that the wife should not leave her husband (but if she does leave, let her remained unmarried, or else be reconciled to her husband), and that the husband should not send his wife away. But to the rest I say, not the Lord, that if any brother has a wife who is an unbeliever, and she consents to live with him, let him not send her away. And a woman who has an unbelieving husband, and he consents to live with her, let her not send her husband away. For the unbelieving husband is sanctified through his wife, and the unbelieving wife is sanctified through her believing husband; for otherwise your children are unclean, but now they are holy. Yet if the unbelieving one leaves, let him leave; the brother or the sister is not under bondage in such cases, but God has called us to peace. For how do you know, O wife, whether you will save your husband? Or how do you know, O husband, whether you will save your wife? (1 Cor. 7:10-16, NASB)

On submission:

Wives, submit to your husbands as to the Lord. For the husband is the head of the wife as Christ is the head of church, his body, of which he is the Savior. Now as the church submits to Christ, so also wives should submit to their husbands in everything (Eph. 5:22-24, NIV).

Who teaches:

Teach the older women to be reverent in the way they live, not to be slanderers or addicted to much wine, but to teach what is good. Then they can train the younger women to love their husbands and children, to be self-controlled and pure, to be busy at home, to be kind, and to be subject to their husbands, so that no one will malign the word of God (Titus 2:3-5, NIV).

On God's Word:

Your word is a LAMP to my feet and a light to my path. I have sworn an oath and confirmed it, to observe your righteous ordinances.... Plead my cause and redeem me; give me life according to your promise (Ps. 119:105, 154, NRSV).

Where to put God's word:

Your word I have hidden in my heart, that I might not sin against You.... This is my comfort in my affliction, for Your word has given me life (Ps. 119:11, 50, NKJV).

Think about God:

I remember the days of long ago; I meditate on all your works and consider what your hands have done (Ps.143:5, NIV).

God's power is in His Word:

For the word is living and active. Sharper than any double-edged sword, it penetrates even to dividing soul and spirit, joints and marrow; it judges the thoughts and attitudes of the heart. Nothing in all creation is hidden from God's sight. Everything is laid bare before the eyes of him to whom we must give account (Heb. 4:12-13, NIV).

Our conduct:

Put these things into practice, devote yourself to them, so that all may see your progress (1 Tim. 4:15, NRSV).

On sacrifice:

By him therefore let us offer the sacrifice of praise to God continually, that is, the fruit of our lips giving thanks to his name (Heb. 13:15).

On the church:

Let us draw near with a sincere heart in full assurance of faith, having our hearts sprinkled clean from an evil conscience and our bodies washed with pure water. Let us hold fast the confession of our hope without wavering, for He who promised is faithful; and let us consider how to stimulate one another to love andgood deeds, not forsaking our own assembling together, as is the habit of some, but encouraging one another; and all the more, as you see the day drawing near (Heb. 10:22-25, NASB).

God's invitation:

Call to Me, and I will answer you, and show you great and mighty things, which you do not know (Jer. 33:3, NKJV).

A woman who longed to be a mother:

Then Hannah prayed and said, "My heart rejoices in the Lord; in the Lord my horn is lifted high. My mouth boasts over my enemies, for I delight in your deliverance...." And the Lord was gracious to Hannah; she conceived and gave birth to three sons and two daughters. Meanwhile, the boy Samuel grew up in the presence of the Lord (1 Sam. 2:1, 21, NIV).

On eternity:

Consequently he is able for all time to save those who approach God through him, since he always lives to make intercession for them (Heb. 7:25, NRSV).

On temptation:

For because He Himself [in His humanity] has suffered in being tempted [tested and tried], He is able (immediately) to run to the cry of (assist, relieve) those who are being tested and tempted and tried {and who therefore are being exposed to suffering] (Heb. 2:18, AMP).

On testing:

For we do not have a high priest who cannot sympathize with our weaknesses, but one who has been tempted in all things as we are, yet without sin (Heb. 4:15, NASB).

About your body:

I will praise thee; for I am fearfully and wonderfully made; marvelous are thy works; and that my soul knoweth right well. My substance was not hid from thee, when I was made in secret, and curiously wrought in the lowest parts of the earth. Thine eyes did see my substance, yet being unperfect; and in thy book all my members were written, which in continuance were fashioned, when as yet there was none of them (Ps. 139:14-16).

Your commission:

Go therefore and make disciples of all the nations, baptizing them in the name of the Father and of the Son and of the Holy Spirit, teaching them to observe all things that I have commanded you; and lo, I am with you always, even to the end of the age (Matt. 28:19-20, NKJV).

God's plan:

For we are God's worksmanship, created in Christ Jesus to do good works, which God prepared in advance for us to do (Eph. 2:10, NIV).

God keeps us to the end:

May the God of peace himself sanctify you entirely; and may your spirit and soul and body be kept sound and blameless at the coming of our Lord Jesus Christ. The one who calls you is faithful, and he will do this (1 Thes. 5:23-24, NRSV).

A Christian need fear nothing:

To him who is able to keep you from falling and to present you before his glorious presence without fault and with great joy—to the only God our Savior be glory, majesty, power and authority, through Jesus Christ our Lord, before all ages, now and forevermore! Amen (Jude 24-25, NIV).

Our hope:

In the future there is laid up for me the crown of righteousness, which the Lord, the righteous Judge, will award to me on that day; and not only to me, but also to all who have loved His appearing (2 Tim. 4:8, NASB).

Our walk through life:

Blessed is the man that walketh not in the counsel of the ungodly, nor standeth in the way of sinners, nor sitteth in the seat of the scornful. But his delight is in the law of the Lord; and in his law doth he meditate day and night. And he shall be like a tree planted by the rivers of water, that bringeth forth his fruit in his season; his leaf also shall not wither; and whatsoever he doeth shall prosper. The ungodly are not so; but are like chaff which the wind driveth away. Therefore the ungodly shall not stand in the judgment, nor sinners in the congregation of the righteous. For the Lord knoweth the way of the righteous; but the way of the ungodly shall perish (Ps. 1:1-6).

An admonition:

My child, keep your father's commandment, and do not forsake your mother's teaching (Prov. 6:20, NRSV).

On discipline of children:

Withhold not discipline from the child, for if you strike and punish him with the [reedlike] rod, he will not die (Prov. 23:13, AMP).

How a child looks at his parents:

Children, obey your parents in everything, for this pleases the Lord (Col. 3:20, NIV).

Wisdom's advice:

Whoever heeds instruction is on the path to life, but one who rejects a rebuke goes astray (Prov. 10:17, NRSV).

Where satisfaction comes from:

The backslider in heart will be filled with his own ways, but a good man will be satisfied from above (Prov. 14:14, NKJV).

On purity:

He who loves purity of heart and whose speech is gracious, the king is his friend (Prov. 22:11, NASB).

On friends:

For if they fall, the one will lift up his fellow; but woe to him that is alone when he falleth; for he hath not another to help him up (Ecc. 4:10).

A directive to those who are in the workplace:

Make it your ambition to lead a quiet life, to mind your own business and to work with your hands, just as we told you, so that your daily life may win the respect of outsiders and so that you will not be dependent on anybody (1 Thes. 4:11-12, NIV).

How to look at the world:

Do not conform any longer to the pattern of this world, but be transformed by the renewing of your mind. Then you will be able to test and approve what God's will is—his good, pleasing and perfect will (Rom. 12:2, NIV).

A remarkable woman in Scripture:

At Joppa there was a certain disciple named Tabitha, which is translated Dorcas. This woman was full of good works and charitable deeds which she did. But it happened in those days that she became sick and died. When they had washed her, they laid her in an upper room. And since Lydda was near Joppa, and the disciples had heard that Peter was there, they sent two men to him, imploring him not to delay in coming to them. Then Peter arose and went with them. When he had come, they brought him to the upper room. And all the widows stood by him weeping, showing the tunics and garments which Dorcas had made while she was with them (Acts 9:36-39, NKJV).

How to overcome problems:

Do not be overcome by evil, but overcome evil with good (Rom. 12:21, NASB).

Do good:

Do not withhold good from those to whom it is due, when it is in your power to do it (Prov. 3:27, NRSV).

The golden rule:

Therefore all things whatsoever ye would that men should do to you, do ye even so to them; for this is the law and the prophets (Matt. 7:12).

On devotion to others:

Be devoted to one another in brotherly love. Honor one another above yourselves (Rom. 12:10, NIV).

A woman God blessed:

So Boaz took Ruth, and she became his wife, and he went in to her. And the Lord enabled her to conceive, and she gave birth to a son. Then the women said to Naomi, "Blessed is the Lord who has not left you without a redeemer today, and may his name become famous in Israel. May he also be to you a restorer of life and a sustainer of your old age; for your daughter-in-law, who loves you and is better to you than seven sons, has given birth to him." Then Naomi took the child and laid him in her lap, and became his nurse. And the neighbor women gave him a name, saying, "A son has been born to Naomi!" So they named him Obed. He is the father of Jesse, the father of David (Ruth 4:13-17, NASB).

Our source of joy:

A glad heart makes a cheerful countenance, but by sorrow of heart the spirit is broken (Prov. 15:13, NRSV).

How to look at your work:

I know that nothing is better for them than to rejoice, and to do good in their lives, and also that every man should eat and drink and enjoy the good of all his labor—it is the gift of God (Ecc. 3:12-13, NKJV).

On troubles:

Even though I walk through the valley of the shadow of death, I fear no evil; for Thou art with me (Ps. 23:4, NASB).

On all those impossible things in life:

Verily I say unto you, If ye have faith as a grain of mustard seed, ye shall say unto this mountain, Remove hence to yonder place; and it shall remove; and nothing shall be impossible to you (Matt. 17:20).

On faith:

Without faith is it impossible to please God, because anyone who comes to him must believe that he exists and that he rewards those who earnestly seek him (Heb. 11:6, NIV).

God's call to those in trouble:

Call upon Me in the day of trouble; I will deliver you, and you shall glorify Me (Ps. 50:15, NKJV).

Where to take your burdens:

Cast your burden on the Lord, and he will sustain you; he will never permit the righteous to be moved (Ps. 55:22, NRSV).

Where God puts our sins:

Who is a God like You, pardoning iniquity and passing over the transgression of the remnant of His heritage? He does not retain His anger forever, because He delights in mercy. He will again have compassion on us, and will subdue our iniquities. You will cast all our sins into the depths of the sea (Micah 7:18-19, NKJV).

Draw near:

Since therefore, brethren, we have confidence to enter the holy place by the blood of Jesus, by a new and living way which He inaugurated for us through the veil, that is, His flesh, and since we have a great priest over the house of God, let us draw near with a sincere heart in full assurance of faith, having our hearts sprinkled clean from an evil conscience and our bodies washed with pure water (Heb. 10:19-22, NASB).

Your fears:

Love is made complete among us, so that we will have confidence on the day of judgment, because in this world we are like him. There is no fear in love. But perfect love drives out fear, because fear has to do with punishment. The man who fears is not made perfect in love (1 John 4:17-18, NIV).

What God has prepared for His people:

But as it is written, Eye hath not seen, nor ear heard, neither have entered into the heart of man, the things which God hath prepared for them that love him (1 Cor. 2:9).

What to hope for:

Nevertheless we, according to His promise, look for new heavens and a new earth in which righteousness dwells (2 Peter 3:13, NKJV).

God's deliverance:

For you, O Lord, have delivered my soul from death, my eyes from tears, my feet from stumbling (Ps. 116:8, NIV).

Jesus' return:

In My Father's house are many dwelling place;. if it were not so, I would have told you; for I go to prepare a place for you. And if I go and prepare a place for you, I will come again, and receive you to Myself; that where I am, there you may be also. And you know the way where I am going (John 14:2-4, NASB).

On suffering:

For I consider that the sufferings of this present time are not worthy to be compared with the glory that is to be revealed to us (Rom. 8:18, NASB).

On enemies:

What shall we then say to these things? If God be for us, who can be against us? (Rom. 8:31)

The character of God, a great assurance:

The Lord, the Lord God, merciful and gracious, longsuffering, and abounding in goodness and truth, keeping mercy for thousands, forgiving iniquity and transgression and sin (Ex. 34:6, NKJV).

Christ is the perfect picture of God the Father:

For in Christ all the fullness of the Deity lives in bodily form, and you have been given fullness in Christ, who is the head over every power and authority (Col. 2:9-10, NIV).

Our source of strength:

The Lord is my strength and my shield; my heart trusts in him, and I am helped. My heart leaps for joy and I will give thanks to him in song. The Lord is the strength of his people, a fortress of salvation for his anointed one (Ps. 28:7-8, NIV).

Get right with God:

The Lord is slow to anger but great in power, and the Lord will by no means clear the guilty. His way is in whirlwind and storm, and the clouds are the dust of his feet. He rebukes the sea and makes it dry, and he dries up all the rivers. Bashan and Carmel wither, and the bloom of Lebanon fades. The mountains quake before him, and the hills melt; the earth heaves before him, the world and all who live in it. Who can stand before his indignation? Who can endure the heat of his anger? (Nahum 1:3-6, NRSV)

On maturity:

May our dependably steady and warmly personal God develop maturity in you so that you get along with each other as well as Jesus gets along with us all (Rom. 15:5, TM).

On mercy:

Therefore be merciful, just as your Father also is merciful (Luke 6:36, NKJV).

Look to God always:

Lift up your eyes to the heavens, look at the earth beneath; the heavens will vanish like smoke, the earth will wear out like a garment and its inhabitants die like flies. But my salvation will last forever, my righteousness will never fail.... For the moth will eat them up like a garment; the worm will devour them like wool. But my righteousness will last forever, my salvation through all generations (Isa. 51:6, 8, NIV).

What Christ did for us:

He himself bore our sins in his body on the tree, so that we might die to sins and live for righteousness; by his wounds you have been healed. For you were like sheep going astray, but now you have returned to the Shepherd and Overseer of your souls (1 Peter 2:24-25, NIV).

Do good:

Therefore, let those suffering in accordance with God's will entrust themselves to a faithful Creator, while continuing to do good (1 Peter 4:19, NRSV).

Behold your God:

But Jesus answered them, "My Father has been working until now, and I have been working." Therefore the Jews sought all the more to kill Him, because He not only broke the Sabbath, but also said that God was His Father, making Himself equal with God (John 5:17-18, NKJV).